www.finishinglinepress.com

Like a Fire

poems by

Ayanna Wimberly

Finishing Line Press
Georgetown, Kentucky

Like a Fire

ACKNOWLEDGMENTS

This collection is a new publication but also, for me, a remnant of an
increasingly distant feeling past. I want to thank the people that I came
across at this time, strangers and intimates, family and friends who
listened to me try to process all this in the best way I knew how. This is a
labor of love and a breath of very crisp air. Controlled fires clearing the
field to decompose what's dead and seed new growth. Thank you for
joining me here.

Publisher: Leah Huete de Maines
Editor: Christen Kincaid
Cover Art: Ayanna Wimberly
Author Photo: Ayanna Wimberly
Cover Design: Elizabeth Maines McCleavy

Order online: www.finishinglinepress.com
              also available on amazon.com

Author inquiries and mail orders:
Finishing Line Press
P. O. Box 1626
Georgetown, Kentucky 40324
U. S. A.

Table of Contents

Ouroboros #1

Who constricts whom? Who constructs?
...A man's plaything.

Who's following
who will lead?
But I am melodrama.

not?
The ability to   feel an orgasm without feeling like
an incomplete woman

Or am I just one-dimensional
It's just another scratch on the surface
on the skin
that is brown
and imperfect
But it keeps warm when I am not
And I can be cold.
[Maybe] I even hatched from a rotten egg
The seed of a wrong fruit
(What is an emotional fuck if not simply embarrassing?)
Is it beneath me? Am I below it?
Even the mist clears eventually
When the sun rises the next morning.

It is he who is to fill me up
literally
metaphorically
But then I'm
never nearly as cerebral as I would like to be.
What is a body in disintegration
if not a pawn?
In here is a frenzy

a voice that cries and leaps
into oblivion

What comes out is not
thoughtful   nor   chaste
                        But I'll be picked off when it's time
                                I'll be picked off <u>and</u> it's time*

I think it's high time   to give
                                                                up
                                                                the charade

                        of the objects
I like the shadows
                                that are irrelevant in light

What is a "love me" fuck if not a hateful one?
                                The cold of your back. The freeze of it all
                                                        The chills
Frills.
                        I like the look of scratches on my skin
                        makes me remember the human being inside

What is a quiet car ride
                                a shadowy encounter

I don't have the look of a woman who sits and contemplates this
Not "sweet-faced" enough.
                                But I am being such a big girl.
                And maybe my silhouette surpasses me
in beauty
                                Shouldn't I be in an early bed
                                                hair wonderfully messed
                        brooding face, illuminated by sunlight
A handsome man's muse
A muse he wishes to not have
                                                or

bellowing in the dim light of a stage,
spidery shadow lashes

               reflected on my cheeks

            rushed by the onslaught of salt water I produce
Naturally
Often.
The fingers. The hands
on my body.
Where do they pull?
Can they feel the warm/the cold I feel?

               So much I feel I have to share, but don't

So I become one-dimensional.
With eyes that I wish could say more
       If someone would catch me not smiling, or laughing
And wonder
        About me.
              Something I don't even like to do.
Needing to feel extraordinary   ≠   Trying to be extraordinary

Apersonwholovesyou—->You—->
              Apersonyoulove——>Whotheylove
Something so D I Z Z Y I N G
              …a man's plaything.
    But it's only the sex again.
          Where my mind wanders.
   And it is straight again
And he is out of me   And those things are too.
      I'll meet them again

      Soon

Ouroboros #2

The mesmerizing thing about it
that is the
Who will love you when
you do all of the things you
yourself
do not like.

       Gettin' older = going down
One day I'll undress out of my clothes
out of my skin
away with the cells and genes
that make me the present person.
And can I even write these things
and have you imagine I've written them?
A quick hit on piano keys
   a raindrop on fallen leaves
      a pressure in your groin
A flip of the coin.
      And when it's finally all mine
      who will be surprised?
When I am a dancer in my own dreams
arabesque, pirouette
pointe.
        Ballerina with her hair pulled back
           or around her shoulders
        or tightened around her neck
Who constricts?
Who constructs?
Who assigns the roles   And which, the upper hand?
Do we assign them to each other?

To ourselves?
And
shouldn't I be in an early bed
the pressure on the groin
an ink mark on the skin
a wrinkle on the hand
Shouldn't I be in an early bed
     the dying sunlight thrown across my face
When he is there, inside, I will think of these things
           All of them while he is there
   Inside.

And Declare Wartime

And so
I wish to pluck the moon—a daisy of fortune
These nonsensical things
and all those pretty things
one must be meticulous with those things.
Too late too late
for the storming of the Bastille.
She who were to lead her revolt
too late for the storming of the Bastille.
Missed that
fateful day
storming
setting fire
rebelling
liberating.

Bonita Bonita Bonita

A heavenly turn-of-the-century diatribe.
She with her raven hair, struck in sable
soft to the touch
but so untouchable that
she is one of the lucky ones.
In those who want to touch
the desire builds
overpowers
and they become rabid
as animals
yet still cannot touch.
It whips up a frenzy
inescapable.
       The shadows of them turning into monsters
     no longer men

            misshapen, grotesque
              when the light
is all gone
under the madness of this one.
But she is perched at her window
brushing her hair
while those who love her   want her   crave her   cherish her
are on fire.
Smell the burning flesh
that does not burn

but welts, rather
slowly
systematically
until a pattern all its own
                    in the skin.

                                   And she will sit
                                   brushing her hair.
                                   And she will weep
                                   because she is running out

            of men
            to love her.
            Want her.
            Crave her.
            Cherish.

Lung

On a rainy day, everyone belongs to each other.
To get you out of your clothes
to have you naked before me
to feel the overwhelming sense of being
completely and indiscriminately
with you.
I hate (myself)
for feeling sorry for (myself)
though I feel sorry
(for myself)
because of this hate of (myself).
I hate
reading these words
knowing that I mean them.
To the depths of my heart
I mean them
From the tips of my fingers
to the balls of my feet
I mean them.
With every single hair on my head I mean them.
Even the ones that fall.

Sometimes I am a painting. A Modigliani nude.
Sometimes I have a body beautiful
sometimes I don't forget.
Sometimes my silhouette surpasses me in beauty
perhaps though
beauty was never mine
to begin with.

Fire in the hall.
I have no idea
what any of this is all about
but I am stuck inside; you see, I can't get out.
And the power is out….   Perfect time for a fire drill.
Threw ashes into the sea…

Kind heart, rabid mind.
Kind heart / rabid mind.
Rabid ass mind.

Psychedelic ramblings
Wanderings. Into the fits of space and come out on the other side
a different organism.
All new cells
a whole new outlook
and brain
and functions.
Strange, beautiful.
Wholly.
Have you ever been experienced?

Membrane

Psychoanalysis
zygote Anna exist
it's a Freudian slip Freudian slip it's an
Electra Complex
for the Electra in You
those oedipal urges
toes edible oranges
The unknown, those forgotten things
things that are forgotten that are worth forgetting
forgetting forgotten things that are worth forgetting
so that they become forgotten
becoming forgotten
as a thing
that is worth
forgetting
so that you forget
And you forget
And it is forgotten
to the unknown.
Subconscious / repression
I want to forget.
Eye won the forfeit.
"I vant to be alone."

Chiaroscuro, Pt. I

There is a lantern
deep inside
the depths of my chest
a place otherwise
dark and scary.
Past the bone
tucked behind the ribcage.
It burns too intensely
for me to handle
so much so
that it welts my insides.
How I wish
I could just
turn off that lantern.

Chiaroscuro, Pt. II

Coquette.
I could be more coquettish.
A brush on the skin
light as a feather.
It makes me shudder
through dimensions
and when I start
my body does not stop.
The frills
chills to the very core of me.
I can hear the beating *bum bum*
of a heart
against the silence of the room.
Is it yours or mine?
Something so euphonious
should be forbidden by law.
Dazzling beyond comprehension
it proves too much for me
I come away from myself
I dance with the rhythm
of the resounding quiet
and yet
I am still.
There is little light
no shadows
no silhouettes devouring each other
just two spirits outside of their shells
cavorting through the air.

Whatever light passes through me
pulls through like a silk sheet
and if I lie here long enough
I'll soon be a mound of mica.
But the lantern yet burns
and welts my insides
and this is a scene I will remember
in the thick of it.

The Free Design

The lens flare.
I am pliable. Sometimes
I am thoughtful.
You and that BOY
sitting on a bed
surrounded
by sketches
sketches of
buildings and houses
sketches
of planes dropping bombs on them
waiting for my turn.
How is it that I listen
without judgment
and it is you
who cannot wait to judge?

Chiaroscuro, Pt. III

If, for me,
to turn off that lantern,
to cut off its glow,
to burn out that bulb
I could take her place
I would die to.
So I know how it feels to not feel it at all.
Here is that chiaroscuro again.
So don't be mean.
Except I am mean to myself
And to you always.
The lantern inside houses a light that emits nothing.
I do not want to think only of myself
but if not,
when should I?
When would a good time be?
Hatched from a rotten egg
seed of a rotten fruit
Blue hues shine through me—
the deepest kind.
The lantern houses a light that emits nothing
yet its glow welts my outsides.
Like the sound of a piano in an empty room
the pang of the keys sticking with age
Press, press, stick, stick
Easy. Time.

Annihilationism

The wicked are utterly destroyed after death
so salvation is the key.
            Knowledge and reality have no objective value;

                        It is what we make it. That's what I was afraid of.
We're not meant to keep in touch
            until the day I die.
            Brassy movements to contrast
                        the legato strokes as if upon a cello
                                    The way in which water moves through a crack
with all the sssssusurrant sound
a denouement
a climax
                        resolution of a mystery

                                    Sometimes that's all there's left to say in love
                        a love that drives,
                                    that inflicts guilt
                                    that welts the insides
                        that burns too intensely to handle

He doesn't know how much he shocks my insides
to a boil and a crisp
up into the airy night sky
heavy with the fumes of smoke like wood burning
The body of some charred creature
Strange elixir dripping from you
A sickly sweet
sensation
in the pit of my stomach.

Like Anthrax

Would you rather have instantaneous or acquiescent love?
Are these the choices?
What is more intensely intoxicating than lying nude with
someone you care for
when limbs touch
euphoria's euphoria
nirvana's nirvana
paradise lost and found, lost
found, lost, found
found, lost
and it goes that way long
after skin brushes skin.
When the memories are resonant
when sensory details
poignant
a good touch is much like
good love
it's purity nearly an affront
Pleasure and agony
two chords that sit so closely together that
when one is pinged, the vibration can be felt in the other
Keenly. Deeply.
I will come undone for you.

Untitled, Body Horror

What if
one day
it weren't so easy
What if, one day
without reason
you found that somehow
you had forgotten
how to walk?
How to spell?
How to write your name?
Was it not enough
then
to simply be a person
for them?
For *them.*
Like flies on a carcass
carcass on a hill of burned sentiments
amassed mildewed streaks of blight
upon the earth.
I feel my body swell and buckle.
If it falls to pieces right now
at least I know
it once stood for something
bigger than myself.

Filles de Belleville

In sepia tone
I watched my maker inch his way toward me.
My end; He danced
His legs jittering back and forth
propelling him left and right.
A fighter jet.
Transfixed as I sat
he stole me in one ephemeral movement.
Pressure on me,
a stone crashing into a calm sea, calm
though a ripple there just under the surface
coming to blows when it hits.
Then, flood.
One I've never felt before.
A flash in the pan
and suddenly
familiar.
A suffocation that felt at once eternal
and disappeared
just as quickly as it came.
Closer, closer
I call him
But now he escapes from me. Flits away into an abyss.
Ladies with much youth.
Much youth
Chastity.
Voices coinciding
Audible billet-doux
just for you.

Just for me, too.
But my shifting dancer Romeo
has taken what's left of me.
Jerking around like a bullet in a metal room
with nowhere to go.
Anxieties convening at night, but sometimes gathering
in pairs
in the brightness of day.
They have much to discuss.

Untitled, Vespertine

Is it something *so good?*
Is it something you just want to get into
just wrap yourself into
get lost there
I want to see its legs
jittering toward me
gaping eyes, hollow
with brightest white scleras
a snowy landscape for me to walk through
A blanket
but with me there
a hematic speck
a blimp on the radar
The shadow of recognition
the glint in an eye
the narrow when it is someone unexpected
unwanted
Cavernous eyes
housing the matter of the world
The wrenching
down on Via Dolorosa
Know that I am not running

Untitled, Smoke & Mirrors

Where is the redamancy
for a person like me

Dessert Her

She is not chosen
but she is the main course for the dining experience.
She is no appetizer, but,
rather,
the thing you eat
the morsel that fills you up
too soon.
Ruins your appetite.
She ruins your appetite.
And it takes a long period to get back.
A hunger
a quench
and around again.
With knives to the tendons
is how I want myself served.

Someone Will Lead You

Who will devour me?
You can even pilfer me.
Pilfer my trust
my innards
offer them for scraps
decide what you'll keep
throw the rest away.
I want to feel the weight of you
on my chest
on my thighs
and on my neck
All is quiet. Quiet now.
And you are special.
You are special and you are wanted.
And that is how you will feel all your life
with me
until it's me
that is dispensable

Epidural

Like a feral wolf clawing its way out of my chest
bursting through the ribcage, its jaw pulled back to reveal
jagged teeth jutting out like shards
a foaming mouth thirsty for spilled blood.

I try to drip it down onto the page.
My body does not handle the overload.
I fall apart. My insides are shredded. There is nothing to be done.

The mending is the mangling.
I roll the rock up the cliff, watch it tumble back toward me
and body does not handle the load.
Though
I want it to devour me.
I want to be devoured by it.
I want to worship at the feet of it
I want to be one in its harem.
I want to be its most beloved concubine.
But it rejects me. I scratch at its door with bloodied finger tips
I scream my throat sore for its embrace, it turns the music louder
Staccato waltz we're doing
each trying to get a leg up
taking turns as the lead
I want it violent.
Lock me up and away. Tell me lies. Deceive me.
Make me reliant on you
and only you. Forever until the end.
So that whenever I feel ill, you are my only medicine.
When you make me ill, you are my only medicine
the mending is the mangling.

Untitled, Bedfellow

Desire.
This skin is too soft and smooth to go a minute untouched.
You deserve this. I deserve this.
You could own it
if only for a while
I give it to you as a gift
though in some place far from here
the word gift can mean poison
I will do you in.
I'll be glad to.

Have I been selfish?

Reverent

I needed to destroy you
I needed to be destructive with you
and needed you to destroy me.
I steered you that way.
You, the lion
I was the stench in your nose
I was the smell of flesh and blood
sweet flesh
sour blood.
Something turned—
Are you sure now?
I wonder why they turn so far
when they're sure of you.
I steered you that way.
And when you penetrated and exposed yourself
to that poison
coursing through
It excited you. Recharged you.
Now that you have pilfered the bits from me
whenever you entered
You are whole.
I packaged the upper hand in laminated paper
and laid it square on your lap.
I steered you that way.
Ktenology is an outdated word
but even still
maybe you have a future in it.

This Ruinous God

Now tell me
how it is possible to love
without the intention to love?
How can you trade off on emotion
Barter off love?
Take this now. For I have no use for it.
This little death that puts the calcium in my bones
makes them strong
harder to break
so more abstract things will break instead.
How does it feel
or,
how should it feel?
Does it hurt?

Then, to myself
It does not always have to hurt.
You do not always have to pick up the burden
of the hurt.
Or the guilt packaged with it.
Peel back the plastic
Now you are new.
Though I still do not know
who takes and who gives.
And who loses the most
and who has the most to lose?
How you can transact with love
And how it can bankrupt you.

This cabalistic act of loving
is so far beyond me
out of my grasp
tight around my body.

I'm proffering mine
my love
to no receiving end.
This celestial hierarchy—
how can you order the angels into castes?
If so,
then I put you in mine.

Bed of Nails

AN EMOTIONAL OR RELIGIOUS FRENZY OR TRANCELIKE
STATE, ORIGINALLY ONE INVOLVING AN EXPERIENCE OF
MYSTIC SELF-TRANSCENDENCE
I like hearing my name whispered in ecstasy I love it I like it I love it

Great Fire

why
is
woman
always
mutilated
in
some
way

What is a soul in disintegration if not a pawn?
I'll be picked off when it's time.
I'll be picked off and now it's time.

Don't even think of trying to find her
she will never be there again.

Untitled, Process

shallow characters
vile people
vile people with no purpose
vile people who are not altogether vile
cleverly vile
the love my loves eventually found
the pearl we buried in the ground
the subjects that make it hard to breathe
the one you'll always have to leave

when the rush is over...

ayanna you dead?

funny you ask.

Ayanna Wimberly is a writer born and raised in Chicago. She took to the written world early in life, penning her first short story when she was 5 years old. She went on to explore other forms of writing, producing and directing a short play at Victory Gardens Theater in Chicago and finding a home in screenwriting while attending New York University for Dramatic Writing. It was there her voice was truly sharpened and is evidenced in part by the chapbook *Like A Fire*. Common themes in Ayanna's writing are detachment, rebirth, intimacy, and sensuality. She lives in Chicago.

CPSIA information can be obtained
at www.ICGtesting.com
Printed in the USA
LVHW031634291120
672957LV00045B/591